ROUGH GUIDE TO PLANNING THE FUTURE

A TOOLKIT TO HELP YOUR COMMUNITY GROUP DISCOVER ITS VISION

By Bill Crooks and Jackie Mouradian

I0448348

Written and illustrated by Bill Crooks and Jackie Mouradian
Graphic design: Lindsay Noble, Holly Risbey
Cover image: By Theodore Scott (Own work)
(https://www.flickr.com/photos/theodorescott) [CC-BY-SA-2.0
(http://creativecommons.org/licenses/by-sa/2.0) or GFDL
(http://www.gnu.org/copyleft/fdl.html)], via Wikimedia Commons

Mosaic Creative
www.mosaiccreative.co.uk
info@mosaiccreative.co.uk
+44 (0) 118 9611359

First edition 2014
ISBN #: 978-1-4716-3351-5

Contents

Note from the authors

Welcome to this resource, and we hope you will find it useful and practical. It has a range of activities for helping small community groups put together their vision for the future. It is based on material used in the urban priority areas of Glasgow and Liverpool as well as material used in a number of overseas cities.

The resource is divided into six sections, which represent the essential stages a group needs to go through in order to construct their vision for the future.

Stage 1 looks at what is a vision and why is it important and explores the value of involving people in planning their own future.

Stage 2 is about celebrating the good things about the community which gives positive energy at the start of the process.

Stage 3 is about gathering information on the needs in the community and highlights the different sources of this information.

Stages 4 and 5 include tools to help you analyse and prioritise this information until you are in a position to turn this vision into a plan which is covered in **Stage 6.**

Stage 7 is about measuring our progress using a few simple questions and tools.

Ideally we would recommend that you have two workshops. In the first workshop you could cover stages 1- 3, then have a period of information gathering. Workshop 2 could be then be spent analysing and prioritising this information and agreeing on your vision. If there is time at the end of this session you could start to form a plan for achieving the vision.

For those of you who are limited to one workshop we would suggest you choose one activity from the celebrating section, do the mapping exercise, prioritising and ranking and then record your vision on the templates provided.

Whatever your time limitations are, it is important that the facilitator reads through all the material to see what needs to be prepared in advance. If you are not going to have time in your session to gather information on your area, it would be a good idea to do some research beforehand.

All the best

Bill Crooks and Jackie Mouradian

STAGE ONE

WHY IS VISION IMPORTANT?

What is a vision and why is it important?

This introductory section highlights the importance of having a vision and the value of involving people in creating a vision.

A vision gives hope for things to be better. When individuals, families and communities have hope they feel they can influence and shape their future for the better.

Visions are often set with a timeframe of 5 – 10 years into the future. Visions are often about ideals and may not always be completely fulfilled within the timeframe, but they help to set a new direction and something to work towards.

"Without vision the people perish."
Proverbs 29:18

"Once you choose hope, anything's possible."
Christopher Reeve

"Vision without action is a dream. Action without vision is simply passing the time. Action with vision is making a positive difference."
Joel Barker

Suggested activity:

1. Ask the group to brainstorm what they think a vision is

2. Write the quotes shown above on to flipchart and compare them to what the group has come up with.

Unlocking potential

Helping a community or community group have a vision has the effect of helping to unlock the potential in people. One of the barriers to this is poverty which can be seen as a series of interlocking factors. Working with communities involves breaking these chains and being aware of how they interact with each other.

Powerlessness

Financial insecurity

Vulnerability

Physical Weakness

Isolation

Discuss with your group which of these aspects of poverty you see in your local community

Unemployment
Low income
No assets

Money spent on destructive practices
- drugs, alcohol etc.

Unable to influence policy or speak for themselves

Lack of self esteem
Exploitation by others
Inability to challenge injustice
Lack of confidence

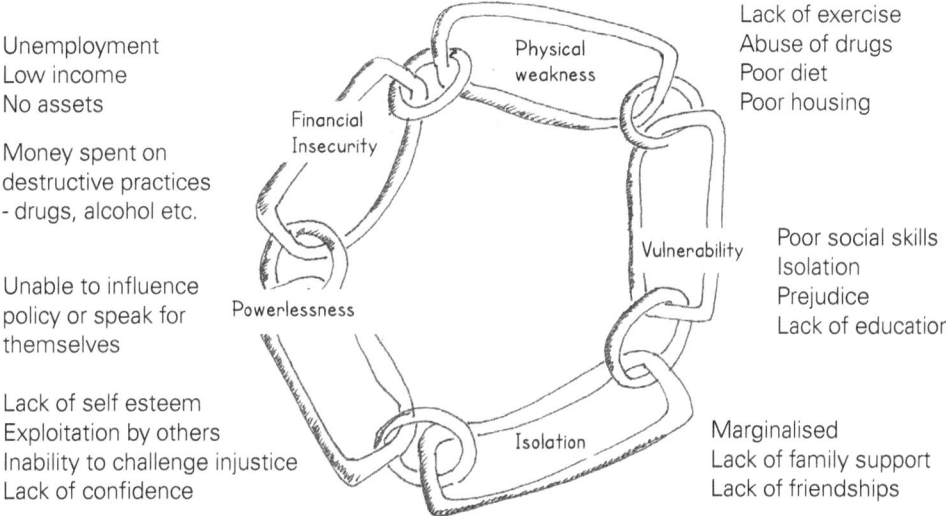

Lack of exercise
Abuse of drugs
Poor diet
Poor housing

Poor social skills
Isolation
Prejudice
Lack of education

Marginalised
Lack of family support
Lack of friendships

> We think sometimes that poverty is only being hungry, naked and homeless. The poverty of being unwanted, unloved and uncared for is the greatest poverty. We must start in our own homes to remedy this kind of poverty.
>
> Mother Teresa

When exploring a vision for your community, it is important to consider the ways poverty can be addressed. Listed below are three ways of breaking the chains. You may want to consider additional ones in your group.

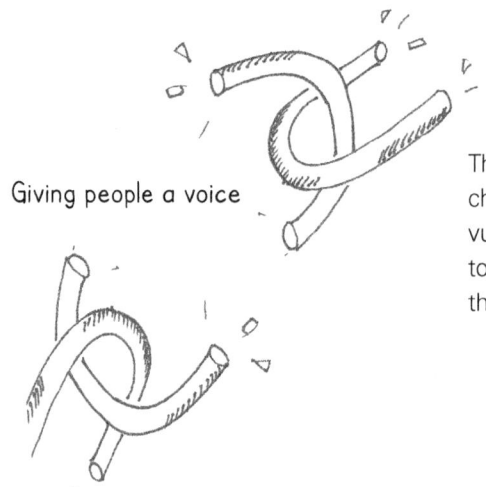

Giving people a voice

This is also about influencing and challenging those who have power over vulnerable people. By giving people a voice to raise their concerns, we are empowering them to take control of their lives.

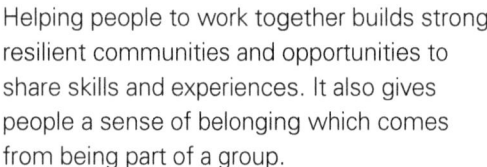

Helping people to work together builds strong resilient communities and opportunities to share skills and experiences. It also gives people a sense of belonging which comes from being part of a group.

A sense of belonging

Good health and well being

Giving people a vision and some hope for the future will improve their sense of well being which in turn, makes it less likely that they will be involved in destructive practices and behaviours.

The importance of involving people

The story of the swing

This story is useful for enabling those involved in designing the vision with the local community to think about the importance of listening to community needs. This has been adapted from materials used by Oxfam in Zimbabwe.

There was once a group of children who played in a park, but there was no swing. So they asked their parents to help them get a swing.

The parents got recommendations from the local authorities... but the children were not impressed!

They then got advice from the Regional Swing Advisory panel ...but the children were not impressed!

Then they got sent recommendations from the All England Panel on Swings and Health and Safety (AEPSHS) ...but the children were not impressed!

The panel referred them to the Executive Swing Council of the European Union...but the children were not impressed!

Finally, a delegation of all the above groups visited the village and asked the children what exactly did they want... and the children drew a picture like this...

Questions

- What are some of the risks of not consulting the people we are trying to help?
- Can we think of examples where people have not been consulted?
- How can we involve people we are trying to help in deciding what the best solutions are?

STAGE TWO

CELEBRATING WHO WE ARE

AND WHERE WE LIVE

Celebration

Sometimes we get bogged down in analysing too much too soon without giving space and time to say what is good and what we can build on. Celebration gives energy, and a sense of excitement and brings communities together.

Sometimes celebration can uncover skills or resources that we did not realise were there.

Why is celebration important?

Lifts our spirits and encourages us

Builds confidence in what we do

Helps us think about our potential as a group to do things together

Helps us to appreciate each other

Helps us realise what we do best

Gives us energy to take on new opportunities

Helps us think about what we could build on

On the following pages, there are two activities to help you celebrate your community. If you have time you could try them both; if not, choose the one you think would suit your group best.

Activity 1: Celebrating our history

Purpose:

To look back at the key events that have shaped the local community and to see what to build on for the future.

Step by step guide

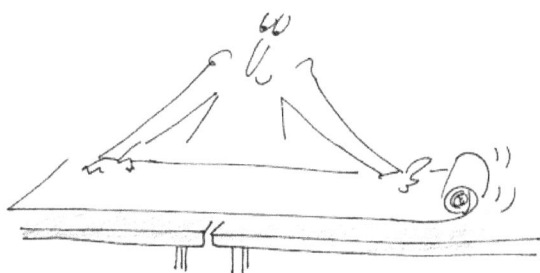

Step 1: Get a piece of lining paper and lay it across some tables with enough room for people to walk round it.

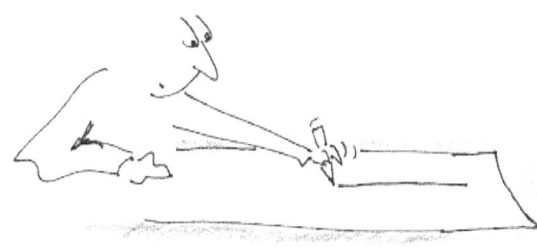

Step 2: Draw a line from one end of the paper to the other and decide the length of time this represents which could be 1 year or 10 years or more.

Step 3: As a group, decide the key events in the order in which they occurred and mark them on the line.

Step 4: Write the things that went well above the line and the things that did not go so well below the line.

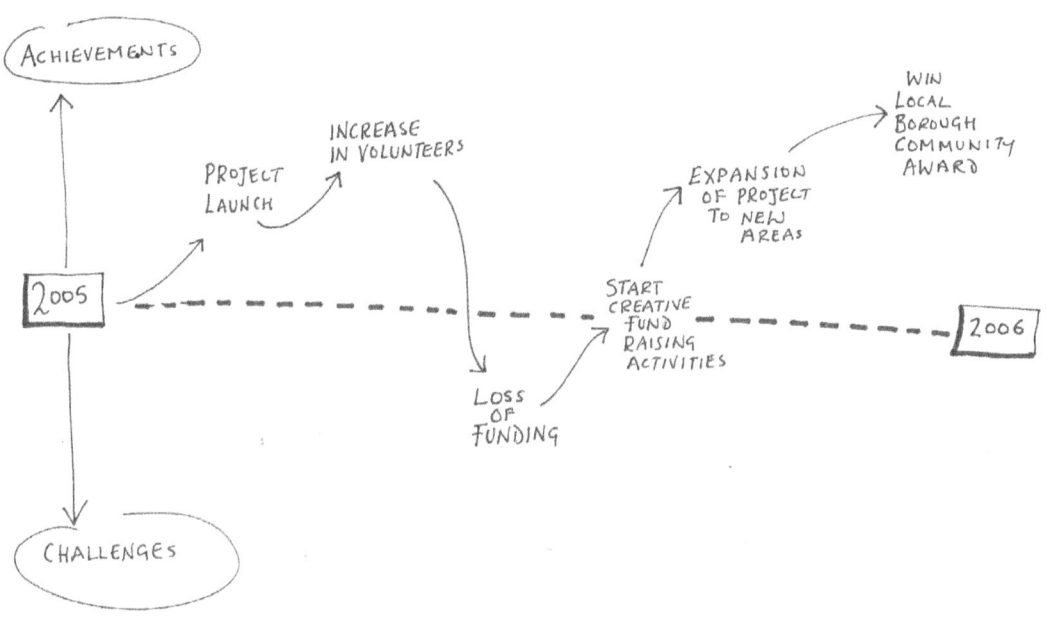

Step 5: Discuss why things went well and other things didn't go so well using the questions on the next page and decide what lessons there are for the future.

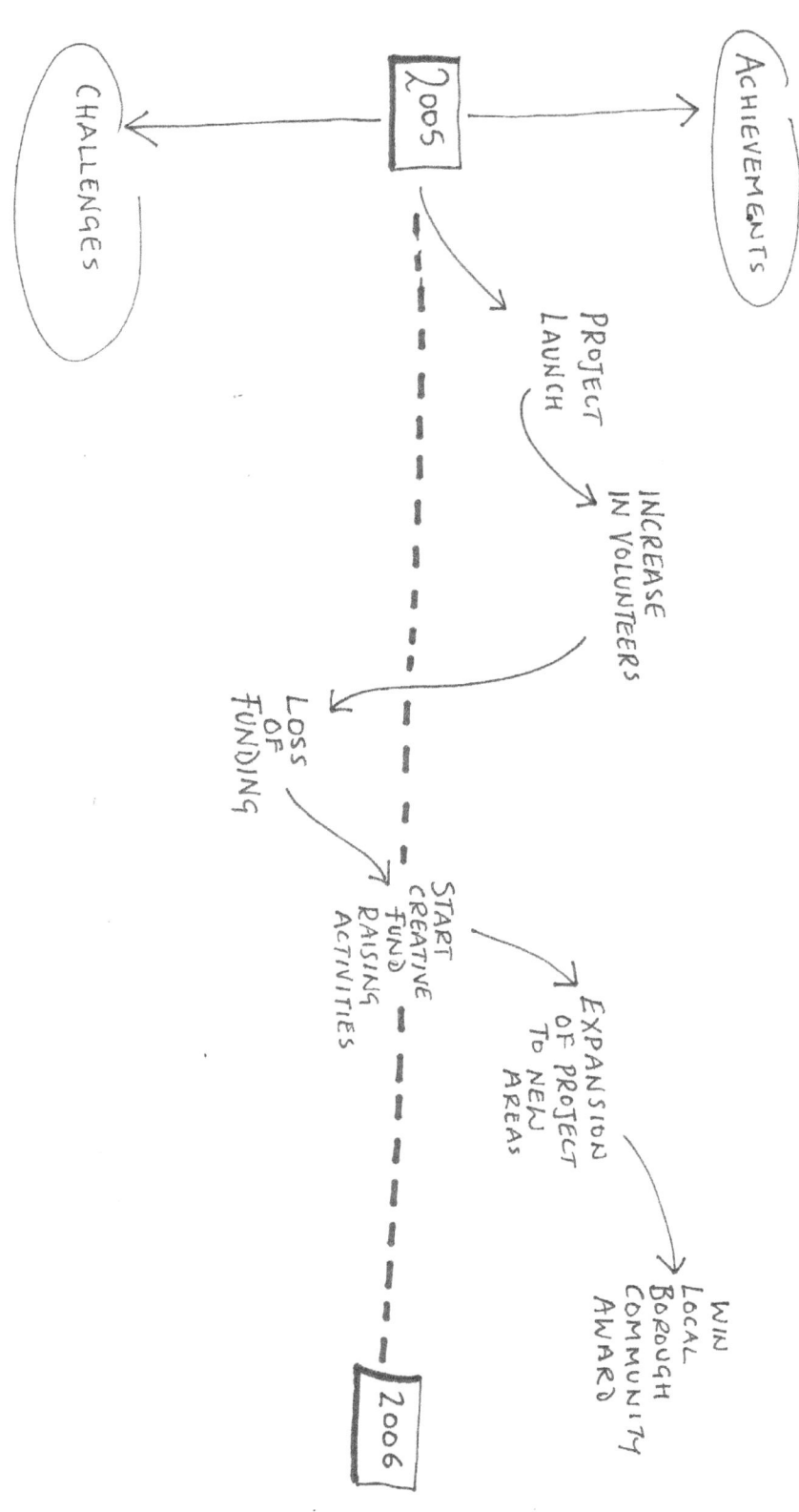

2005

ACHIEVEMENTS

CHALLENGES

PROJECT LAUNCH

INCREASE IN VOLUNTEERS

LOSS OF FUNDING

START CREATIVE FUND RAISING ACTIVITIES

EXPANSION OF PROJECT TO NEW AREAS

WIN LOCAL BOROUGH COMMUNITY AWARD

2006

Questions

What have been the best moments and why?

What has been most challenging?

What can we build on for the future?

Tips for running this exercise

Time required: 50-60 mins

Materials required: Roll of lining paper from the DIY shop, marker pens, newspapers and / or magazines

Tips:

You could use pictures from magazines or newspapers to illustrate the events on the timeline.

1. Alternatively, just draw pictures.

2. If there is a large group (more than 10) make sure everyone can see the timeline and can contribute. Otherwise do 2 or 3 groups and compare timelines at the end of the session.

3. It is important as a facilitator to keep the momentum of the activity going and not to get too stuck on one particular event. It is also important to explore with the group why an event was good or bad and what lessons or insights have they gained from it to apply to the future.

Activity 2: Celebrating with pictures

Purpose:

To help the group appreciate the good things about their community.

Step by step guide

Step 1: Split into small groups, depending on the size of the group, to discuss what people appreciate about their community.

Step 2: Provide a selection of magazines and newspapers for the groups to look through.

Step 3: The community members cut out suitable pictures which reflect the things they appreciate and create a collage.

Step 4: Each group shares their pictures with the rest of the group.

Step 5: The facilitator groups the pictures and then everyone discusses the three questions.

Step 6: Summarise the activity and help the group identify 3 actions they could do as a result of this exercise.

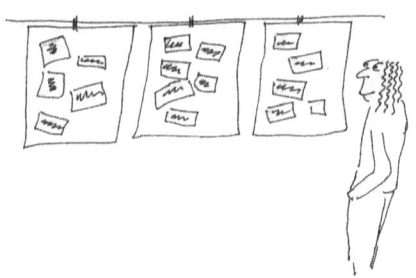

Questions

What are the common themes?

What could we build on?

Which areas give us the most energy?

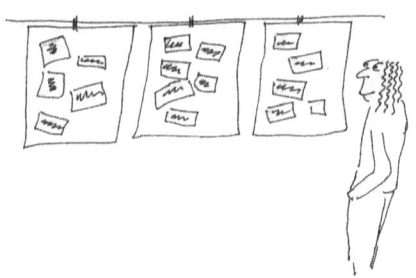

Worked example

Tips for running the exercise

Time required: 1 hour – 1 hour 10 mins

Materials required: Pile of varied magazines and newspapers (old catalogues are good value too)

Glue, scissors and sheets of flipchart paper to stick the pictures on, marker pens and masking tape or clothes pegs and a washing line to hang the pictures on.

Tips:

1. Make sure the small groups have had time to discuss the things they are proud of before they have the magazines (otherwise they may start reading the magazines before they know what the task is).

2. If possible try to put the small groups around some tables and not more than 4-5 in a group.

3. Monitor the progress of the group and give them a five minute warning before the time of giving feedback.

4. Invite the groups to comment on each others' posters.

5. When discussing the questions, form a large circle to create a more focused environment.

STAGE THREE

GATHERING INFORMATION

Gathering information

Once you have identified what's good about your community and what you have to build on, it is time to look at the various issues and needs. For this you will need to do some research. Gathering information involves collecting information from three sources.

The first source is the community themselves or the groups you are directly involved with. When gathering information, try to explore with them the key challenges of their situation and their hopes for the future.

The second source of information is usually from people who know about the community but do not necessarily live in it. This could include social workers, community workers, teachers and police, doctors.

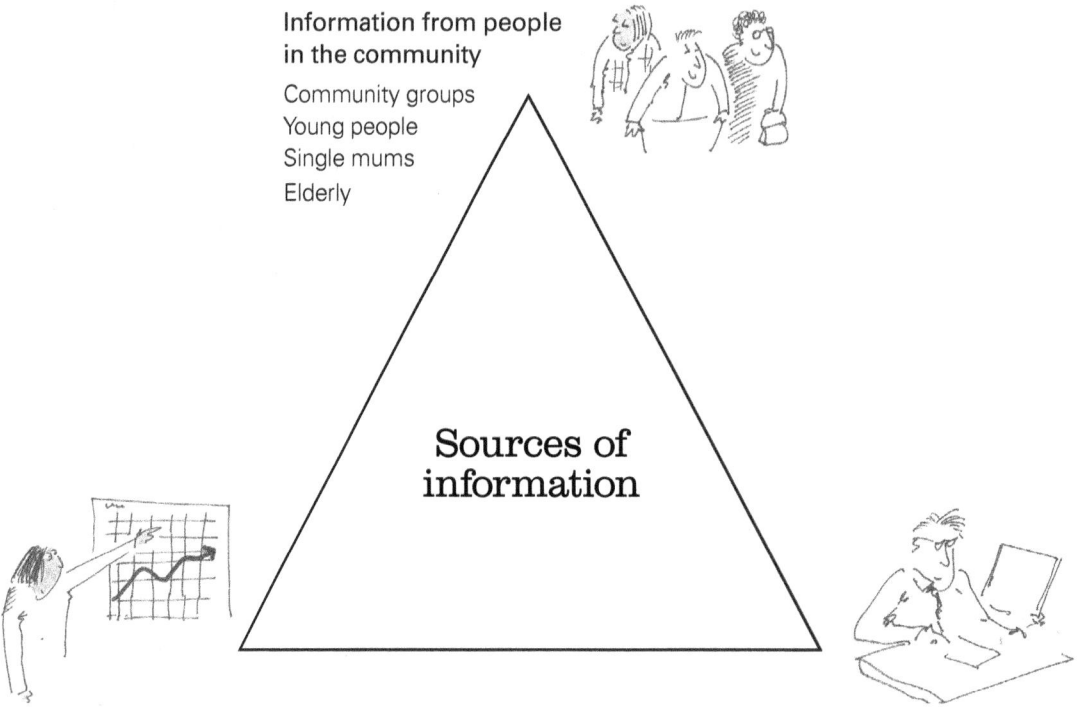

Information from people in the community

Community groups
Young people
Single mums
Elderly

Sources of information

Information from key workers in the community

Clergy
Social workers
Community Wardens
Community Leaders

Information from statistics

Drug and alcohol statistics
Crime figures
Teenage pregnancies
Demographics
Number of school leavers
Homelessness

The third source of information is statistics which can be found on the web and can relate to the exact postcode in which the community or community group are located. This gives statistical information about levels of crime, literacy, drug addiction and substance abuse, overall health and mortality rates.

A useful website for these statistics is **www.neighbourhood. statistics.gov.uk**, where you can select information for your town, just for your council ward or, if you want to know about your own local neighbourhood, then choose 'Super Output Area' from the list.

Think about what information is most likely to be of importance to the particular group you are working with and select some key bits of data.

Gathering information from community members

There are a number of tools for gathering information but one of the simplest and most effective ways is to get groups to create a map of their area. This can be a form of focus group and is a good way of getting people involved in thinking about the current issues they face and how they would like their community to look in the future.

Mapping

Mapping can be done at two levels; either within local communities which may involve a few streets, or it can be done across a town for groups that are involved in networks that cover the area. This may involve identifying the key areas of poverty or deprivation and then highlighting the areas where an organisation or network is currently involved and where the gaps are in relation to areas of poverty.

Step by step guide

Step 1: Put some large tables together and put together 4-6 pieces of flipchart on which to draw a map.

Step 2: Mark on the map in marker pen, the main roads, rivers, railways etc.

Step 3: Mark on the map key buildings such as shopping centres, churches, mosques, pubs, clubs, etc.

Step 4: Discuss and mark on the map the main areas of need or concern to the community.

Step 5: Give each person 10 coloured sticky labels. They can then choose how many labels they would put on a specific need.

Step 6: Count up the sticky labels and see which are the top 3- 5 priorities (depending on how many you have) and list them on a flipchart.

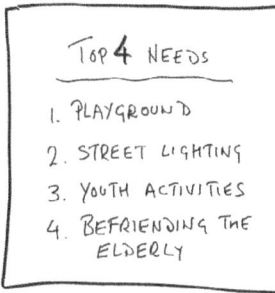

Step 7: Of the top priorities listed discuss which of them can be done by the community.

Maps from different peer groups

Another way of doing this exercise is to give different peer groups the task of drawing a map of the same area which will give you 3 different perspectives and insights into the needs of the community.

Single mums   The elderly   Young people

Once the map has been analysed and discussed, a final version can be produced as a way of visualising what initiatives could be done in the community over the next one to two years.

Tips for running the session

Time required: 45-1 ½ hours depending on the size of the group

Materials: Marker pens, plenty of flipchart paper, masking tape to stick the flipchart paper together, crayons to highlight and colour the map, coloured sticky labels.

Tips

1. If there is a large group, subdivide it so there are smaller groups working on a number of maps. Bear in mind this will demand a longer time for feedback.

2. Sometimes it is quite useful to divide the group according to age, gender and marital status eg, young people, pensioners, single mums and asylum seekers.

3. It is best to draw the roads and communications on first as this helps to locate other items on the map.

4. To enhance this activity even more you can encourage a group to take some photographs of their community.

5. The map can become an important source of planning in the future so if possible, put it up in a place where people can see it and add to it.

6. In a different colour pen you could mark on the map some of the good things about the area that you identified in the celebration stage. This may help when you start to think of ways of addressing the issues.

Worked examples

Local area community map

This is done by a local community group or groups, who identify problem areas and rank them according to priority.

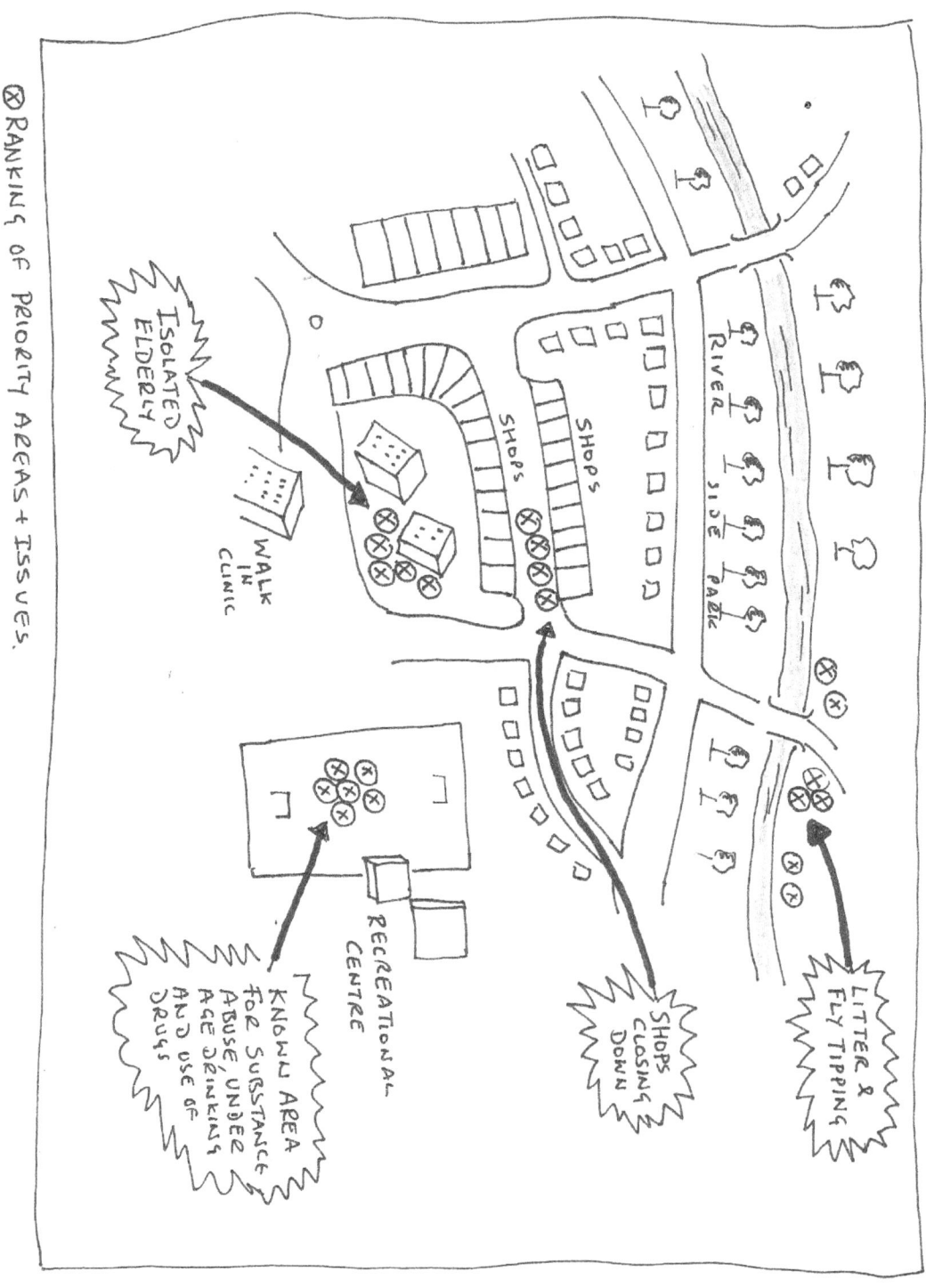

Town wide map

This is done by an organisation or institution who mark on the map the areas of poverty and deprivation and also the areas where it is currently working which in turn identifies the gaps in provision and support.

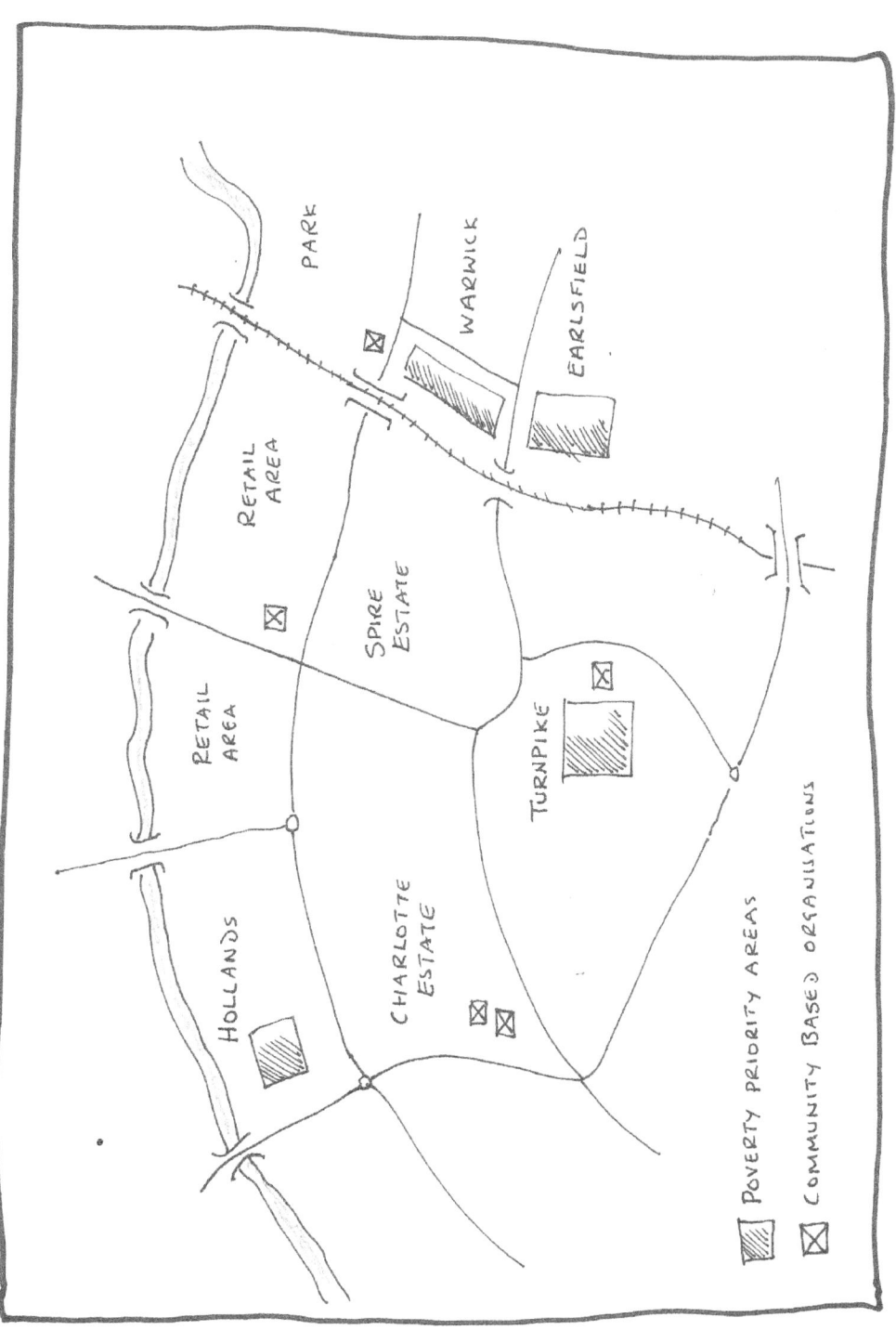

Who does what in your community?

This is a short exercise which tries to identify who is currently doing what in our community. This helps us in two ways:

- It helps us see what additional resources we might have to build on to achieve our vision.

- It stops us duplicating something that might already be there and also helps us see who else we could work with in achieving the vision.

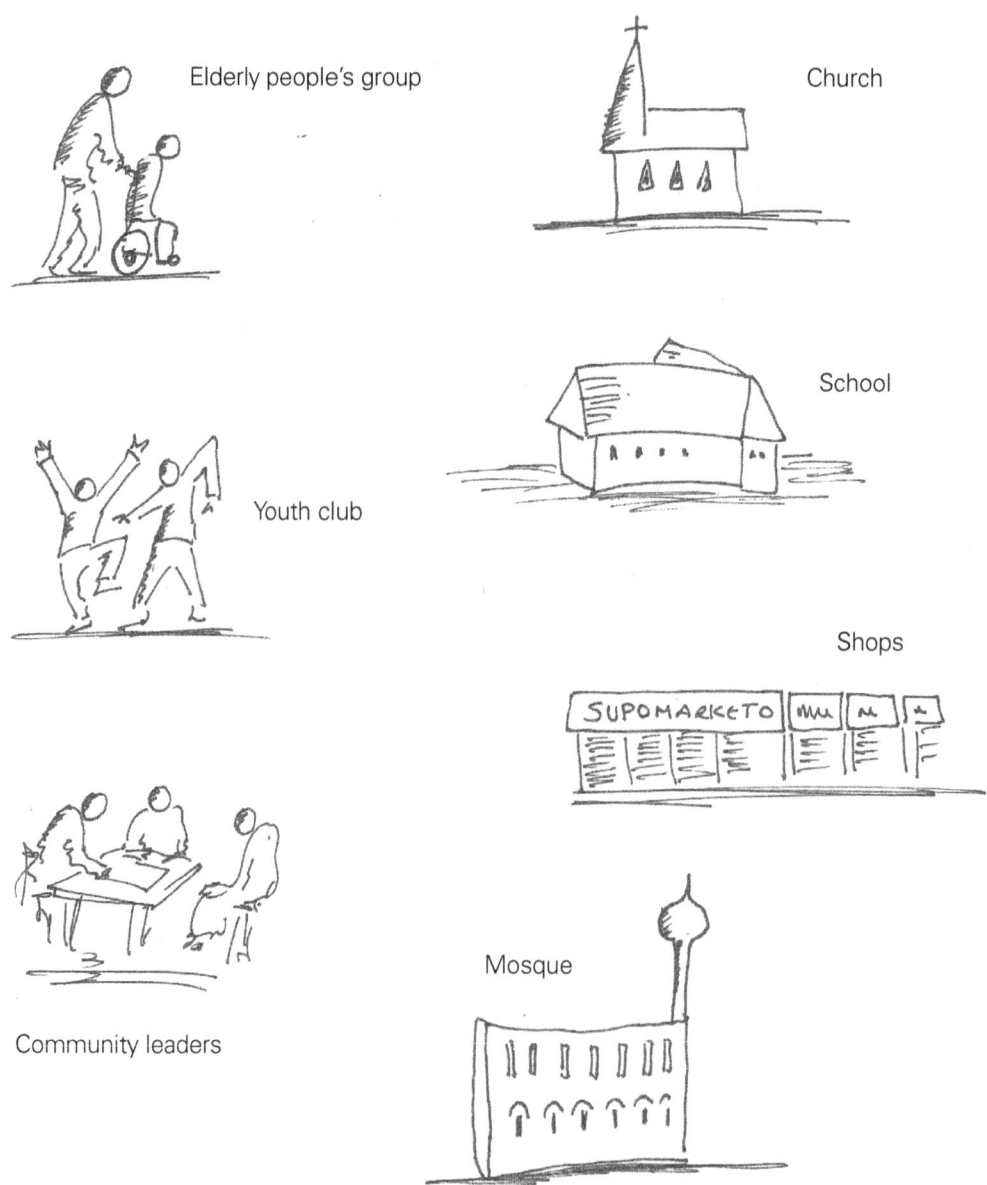

Elderly people's group

Church

School

Youth club

Shops

Community leaders

Mosque

Make a list of all the institutions and groups that are represented in your community as shown in the example on the previous page. Draw a bigger version of the table below and fill it in.

Institutions and groups	What do they do?	How might we work with them?

Discuss what services and support each institution or group offers to the community and how you might work together with them.

STAGE FOUR

ANALYSING INFORMATION

Problem Tree

Once you have gathered the information it is important to look at the common themes. With each of these themes, it can be useful to use a problem tree to analyse these themes in more detail. This helps a community or community group to think how they can respond appropriately as well as think about their vision for the future in addressing one or more problems.

Step by step guide

Step 1: Identify a problem that the group would like to analyse in order to respond to it. Draw a tree on a large piece of paper.

Step 2: Explain that the trunk of the tree represents this problem. The leaves of the tree represent the symptoms of the problem and the roots represent the root causes.

Step 3: As a group identify the symptoms of your chosen problem and write these on the leaves of the tree or on post-it notes. A good way of doing this is to think of a symptom and then ask 'what does this lead to?' And you will get a further symptom and so on (see worked examples).

Step 4: Similarly, identify the root causes as a group and write these on the roots of the tree. A good way of doing this is to think of a cause and then ask 'why is that?' and you will get a deeper cause, and so on (see worked examples).

Step 5: Discuss whether your group and community should be addressing a root cause or a symptom of the problem.

In general, addressing a symptom is much easier, but is often only a short term solution.

Addressing a root cause is often more challenging but may bring about lasting change.

Worked example – Youth crime

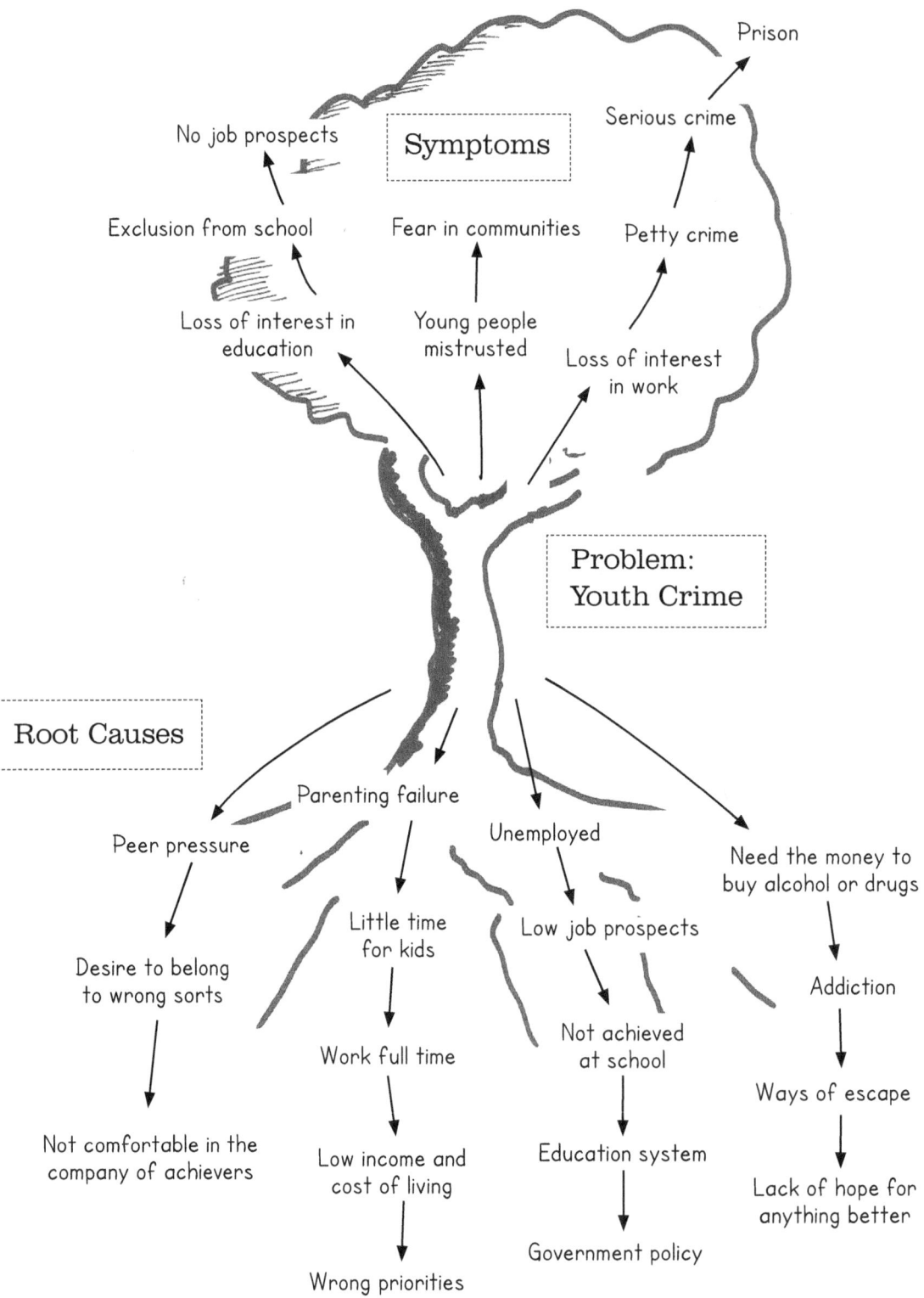

Prison

Serious crime

No job prospects

Symptoms

Exclusion from school

Fear in communities

Petty crime

Loss of interest in education

Young people mistrusted

Loss of interest in work

Problem: Youth Crime

Root Causes

Parenting failure

Unemployed

Peer pressure

Need the money to buy alcohol or drugs

Desire to belong to wrong sorts

Little time for kids

Low job prospects

Addiction

Work full time

Not achieved at school

Not comfortable in the company of achievers

Low income and cost of living

Education system

Ways of escape

Government policy

Lack of hope for anything better

Wrong priorities

Worked example – Isolated Elderly

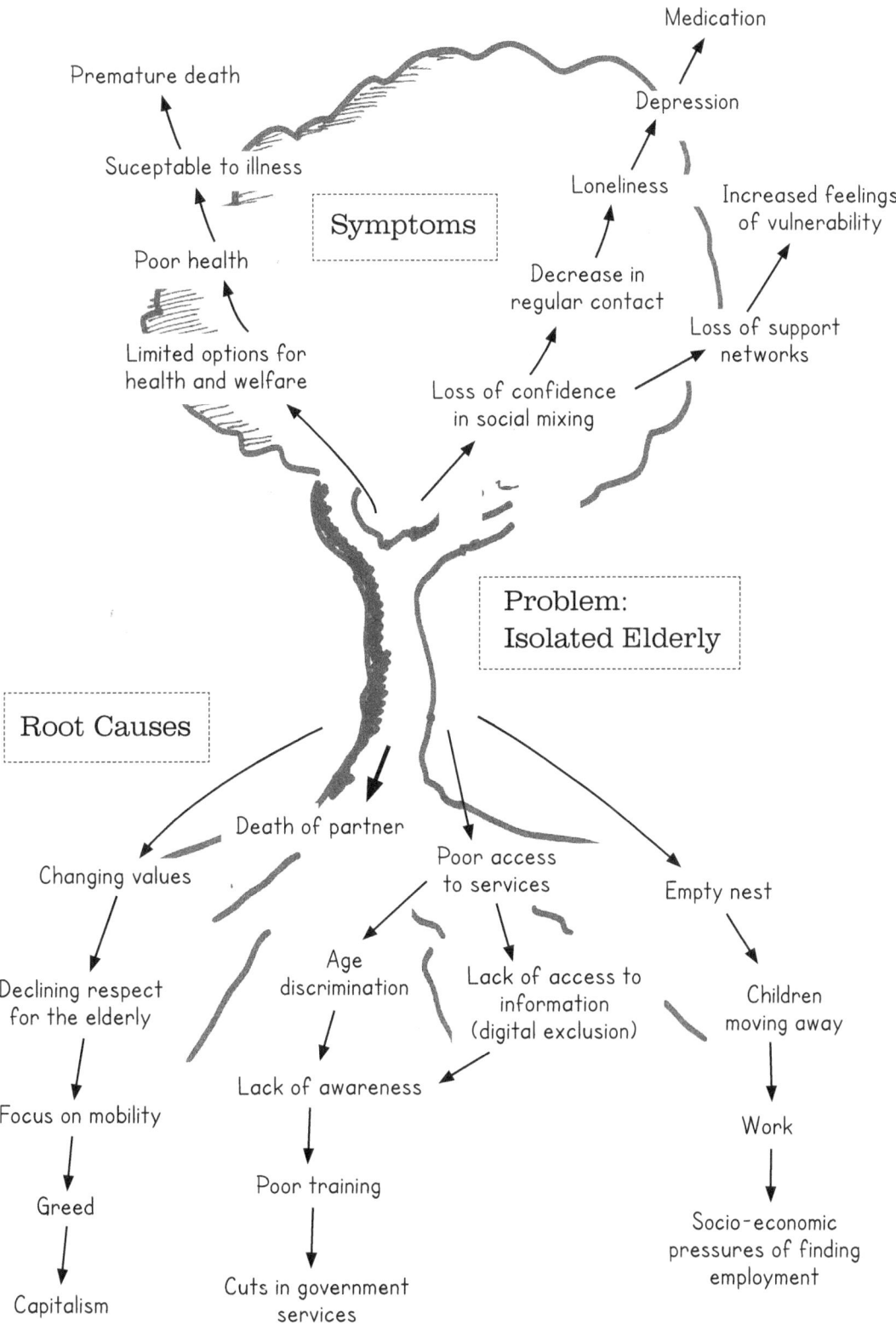

Premature death

Medication

Suceptable to illness

Depression

Symptoms

Loneliness

Increased feelings
of vulnerability

Poor health

Decrease in
regular contact

Limited options for
health and welfare

Loss of support
networks

Loss of confidence
in social mixing

Problem:
Isolated Elderly

Root Causes

Death of partner

Poor access
to services

Empty nest

Changing values

Age
discrimination

Lack of access to
information
(digital exclusion)

Children
moving away

Declining respect
for the elderly

Lack of awareness

Focus on mobility

Poor training

Work

Greed

Capitalism

Cuts in government
services

Socio-economic
pressures of finding
employment

Questions

- Which areas of the tree are other voluntary agencies working with?

- Which part of the problem do you think we would be best suited to work with? (symptoms or causes)

- What sort of project could we do with our skills, knowledge and experience?

- Are there others we could work together with on this?

- What additional resources might we need to do this work?

- If the answers to most of these questions are negative, maybe you need to take another issue and construct another tree.

STAGE FIVE

PRIORITISING AND RANKING

Ranking Priorities

Once you have drawn some community maps, looked at some local statistics and met with groups, you can now consider all the information in terms of themes and prioritise them.

The first step is to draw a table like the one below and then list the various issues under the priority descriptions in the first column. Next, discuss what is your capacity to respond to these needs as a group or community and list the action you would take in the second column. It may be helpful to refer to the strengths identified in the celebration stage when considering your capacity to respond.

Once this has been done, the group can then rank them according to what they consider are the top priorities to be addressed in the third column. This can be done by giving each person in the meeting 5 votes which could be represented by post-its or sticky labels. They can cast all their votes on one priority or spread them across a number of priorities. Then count up all the votes and see if there are three top priorities which can be explored as part of a vision for the future.

Priority Description	Our capacity to respond	Ranked priorities
Vandalism	If the vandalism is due to youth – we could direct young people to youth clubs in the area which might be able to help.	1. Isolation of elderly 2. Vandalism 3. Poor street lighting
Isolation and loneliness of elderly	We could direct old people to local lunch clubs run by different groups including faith groups.	
Poor street lighting	Have good relationship with local councillor who could lobby on our behalf.	
Family debt	No experience in this area – no capacity so need outside external help.	
Drugs and substance abuse amongst young people	Limited experience of dealing with this through youth clubs. Need outside help to set up detached street programme for young people	

Listing priorities ready for ranking

Sharing priorities from the mapping exercise

Sharing priorities from key workers in the community

Sharing priorities from neighbourhood statistics

In the light of the priorities identified above, invite the group to dream about what their ideal community would be like in ten years time. For this, you could invite the participants to close their eyes for 5-10 minutes and dream. Once they've done this, invite them to brainstorm what they've dreamed on to flipchart paper. The more artistic could draw their dreams. Group the brainstorm and pictures into common themes which then could be summarised as a vision for their community.

For example: To make this community an attractive and safer place for all ages, and a place where people want to live together.

Testing the vision

Once a vision has been thought about and written up, it can be useful to test it with a wider group of people or a greater representation from the community. This is important as it creates an opportunity to see if the vision is appropriate to what local people want and in doing this, you can enhance the vision and create ownership of it.

The Swimming Pool

Step by step guide

1. Make signs of the different areas of a swimming pool using pictures from the internet and place them around the room in the order shown on the next page.

2. Explain how the areas of the swimming pool relate to different levels of commitment as described on the next page.

3. Invite the group to go and stand where they think they are in relation to their commitment to the new vision.

4. Go round the group and ask each person to say briefly why they chose to stand where they did. After a number of people have spoken, ask if anyone wants to change their position.

5. Explore with the group what this might mean for them in taking the vision further.

Area of swimming pool	Stage of commitment
Car Park	No commitment at all
Reception	Vague interest
Changing rooms	Interested but needs more information
Toddler pool	Tentatively committed

Shallow end	Committed but wants to see it in action before throwing their lot in
Deep end	Committed and wants to get on with it
Flume	Can't wait to get going - excited - this is what we've been waiting for.

STAGE SIX

TURNING THE VISION INTO A PLAN

Turning the vision into a plan

Once the group have decided on a vision, the next stage is to turn it into a plan that is practical and easy for everyone to understand. A common problem with visions is that no-one really thinks through how they are are going to be achieved.

The Hot Air Balloon

The following exercise is designed to help a group think through the practical realities of putting a plan together. This can be done as a group and documented in such a way that everybody can understand it. The parts of the hot air balloon represent the core of any plan that is going to turn a vision into practical action and deals with the essential questions of what, why, how and who. The other features of the balloon below represent things that might threaten the plan or undermine it. It is good to think about these threats at the planning stage so you can think of ways to address these risks to the success of the project.

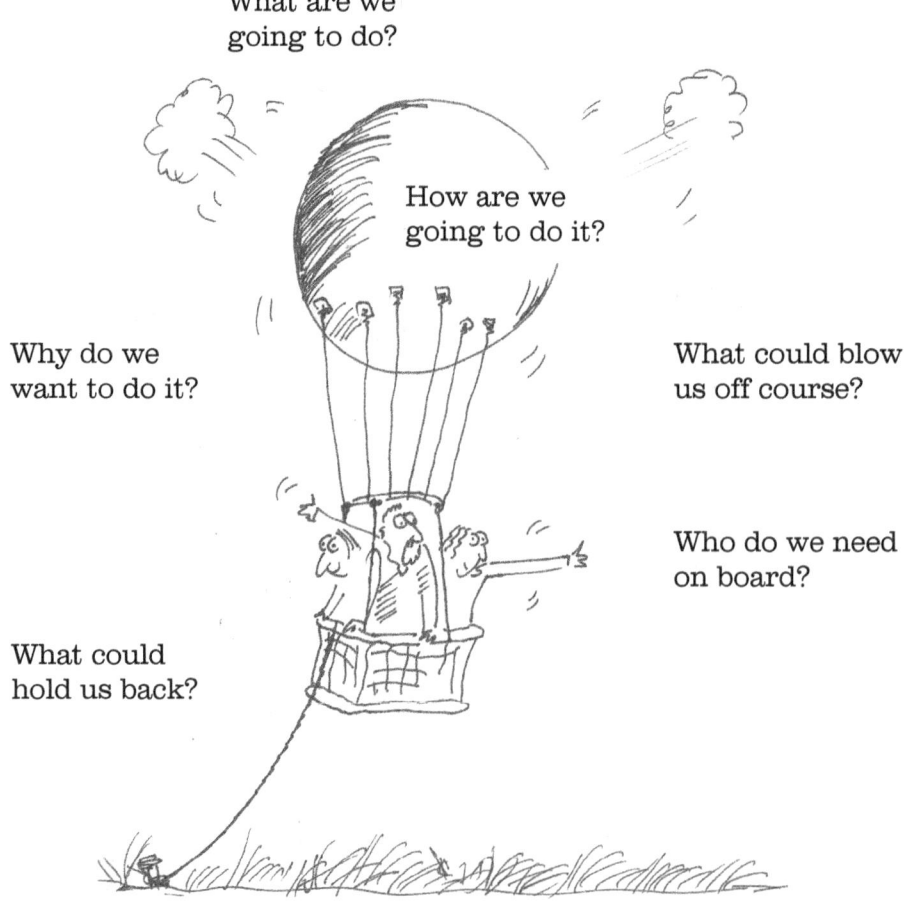

What are we
going to do?

How are we
going to do it?

Why do we
want to do it?

What could blow
us off course?

Who do we need
on board?

What could
hold us back?

Hot Air Balloon

Step by step guide

Step 1: Use the example on the next page to explain how the balloon can be used for turning a vision into a plan.

Step 2: Give everyone post-its and get them to brainstorm each part of the balloon, which relates to the plan.

Step 3: Using the example, get them to discuss what factors may hold them back and blow their activities off course once the plan is underway.

Step 4: Discuss how these threats could be addressed

Step 5: If your vision is quite big and complicated, you can break it down into short term (1-2 years), medium term (3 to 5 years) and long term (6 to 10 years). You could use a separate balloon for each of these time frames.

Hot Air Balloon worked example 1

This example is for a community wide vision. On the following page there is an example for a more specific initiative which could be part of the community wide vision.

What are we going to do?

Make this community an attractive and safer place for all ages and a place where people want to live together

Why do we want to do it?

Because the local community have become increasingly concerned about the level of deprivation in the area and the loss of community spirit

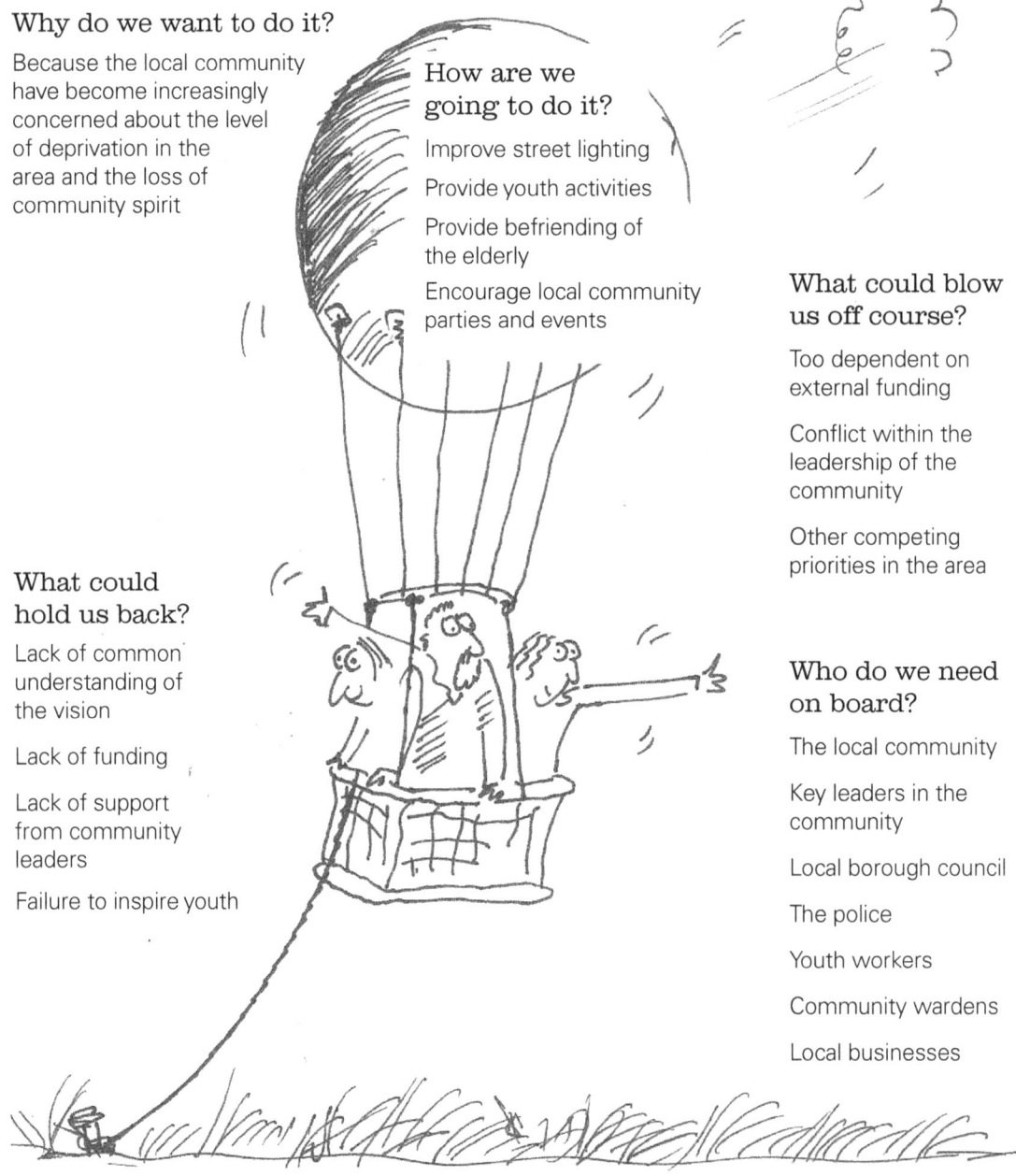

How are we going to do it?

Improve street lighting

Provide youth activities

Provide befriending of the elderly

Encourage local community parties and events

What could blow us off course?

Too dependent on external funding

Conflict within the leadership of the community

Other competing priorities in the area

What could hold us back?

Lack of common understanding of the vision

Lack of funding

Lack of support from community leaders

Failure to inspire youth

Who do we need on board?

The local community

Key leaders in the community

Local borough council

The police

Youth workers

Community wardens

Local businesses

Hot Air Balloon worked example 2

What are we going to do?

Befriend the young people in a local hostel for homeless young people

Why do we want to do it?

There is no local provision for mentoring young homeless people. Youth mentoring is known to have a powerful influence on helping young people make positive choices.

How are we going to do it?

Recruit volunteers

Train volunteers in mentoring skills and ensure safeguarding procedures are in place

Set up a rota and procedures with local authority

Design a programme of regular activities including trips to climbing wall, film nights, games nights etc

Plan regular reviews with stakeholders to see how it's going and what we can learn for the future

What could blow us off course?

Volunteer burn out

Conflict between hostel staff and volunteers

Change in local authority policies – (increase in bureaucracy)

What could hold us back?

Lack of volunteers

Too many competing demands

Lack of local authority support

Lack of interest by the young people themselves

Who do we need on board?

Hostel staff

Local authority representatives

Volunteers

Volunteer coordinator

Homeless young people

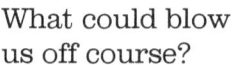

Who can we work with to achieve our vision?

The different aspects of your vision identified by the balloon exercise can then be placed on the following triangle to identify who can be involved in which aspect of your vision.

The top section looks at what external resources might the community need to achieve its vision. This could include external grants and funding and/or political support from the local borough council or other authorities.

The middle section looks at what groups can do together because they can share resources and as a result make a bigger contribution to improving the community.

The bottom section represents individual things community groups can do for themselves in the community. This might relate to their specialist interest areas such as working with the elderly, working with young people.

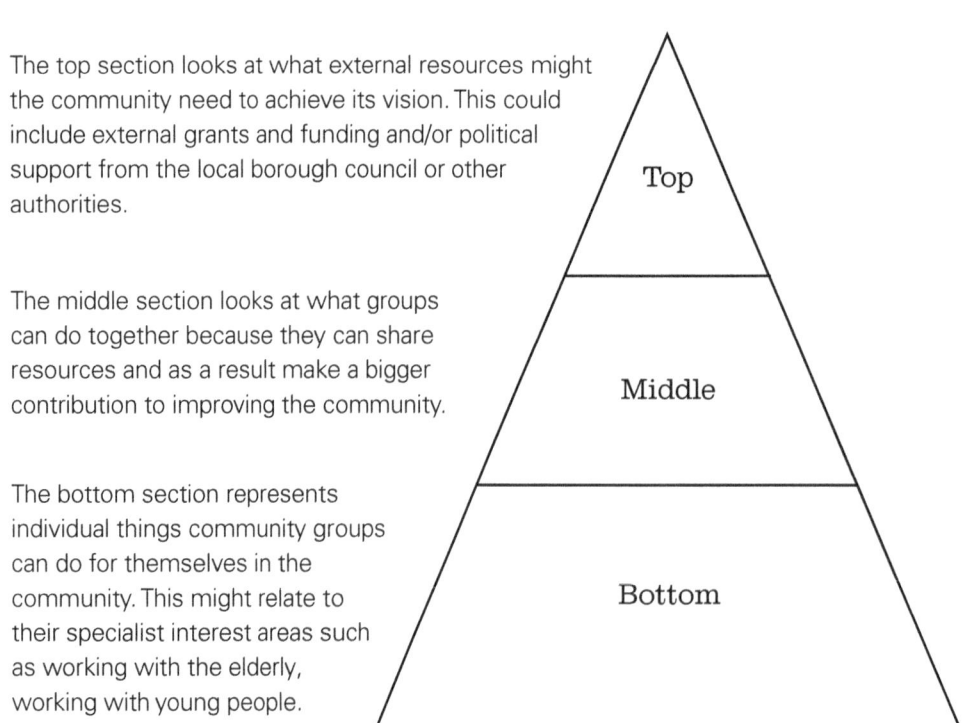

Documenting the vision

This table is designed to help you document the vision you have developed so that you can have a record of it. You can use this to formulate a proposal for your local authority or other funding body.

What priorities have we identified?	
What is our vision?	
Why is it important?	
What are the key elements to it?	
How are we going to achieve it?	
Who do we need to work with?	
What are some of the barriers to achieving the vision and how could they be addressed?	

What have we learnt together in developing the vision?

It is always a good idea to review how your group approached and managed the planning process. Below are a list of questions to help you draw lessons from your experience, which you can use to improve the way you work in the future.

1. What have we achieved?

2. Which bits of this process worked best?

3. What was most challenging?

4. What could we have done better?

5.   How well did we work as a group?

6. How confident do we feel about achieving the vision?

7. Is there anything else we could do to strengthen or support it?

8. How shall we present it to others and keep it alive and inspiring?

STAGE SEVEN

MEASURING OUR PROGRESS

How is it going?

Once you have started your initiative or project, it is important to think about how you will assess its progress and check it is having the impact you intended it to have.

This section looks at some simple questions and tools for measuring progress and change.

The example of a balloon travelling on a journey is a good way of thinking about the basics of monitoring and evaluation.

Below are some questions you might ask during the course of running a project.

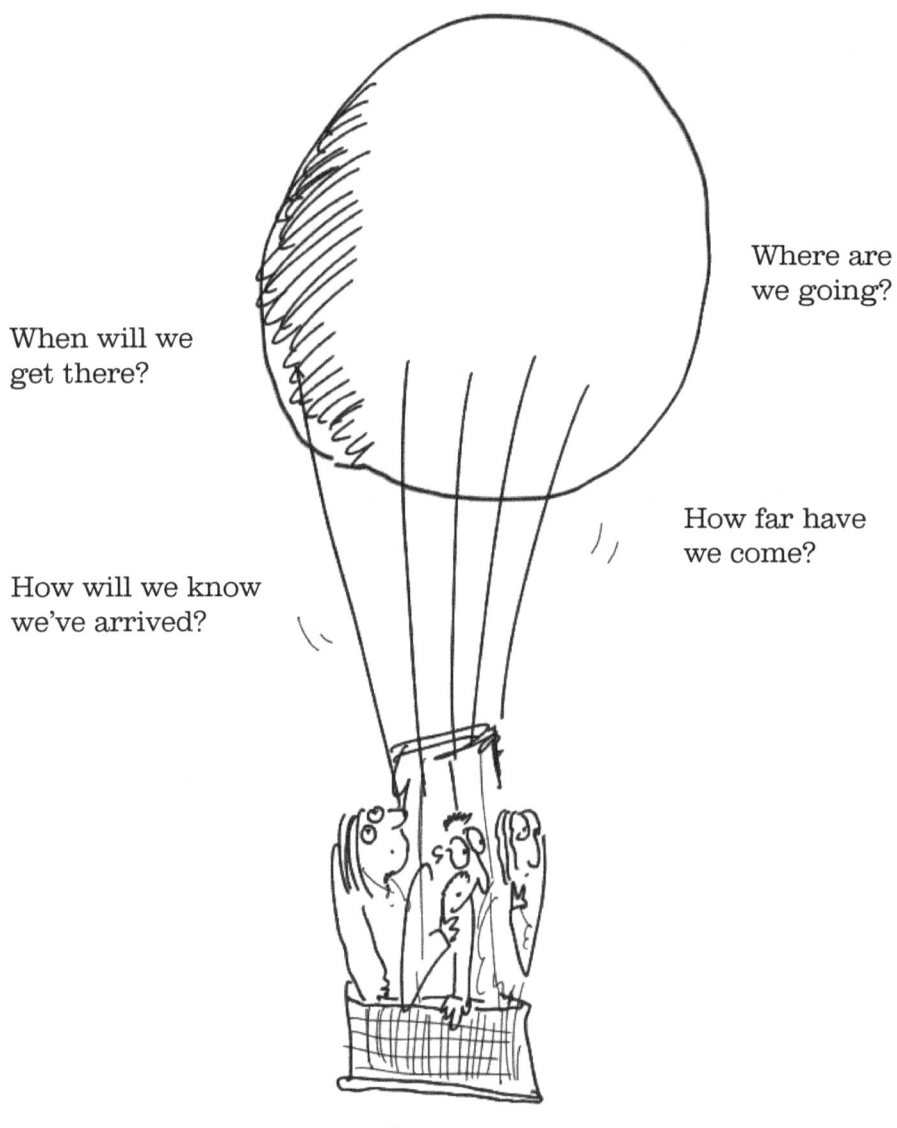

Where are
we going?

When will we
get there?

How far have
we come?

How will we know
we've arrived?

Monitoring is really useful as it provides lots of information that can be reviewed at the end of the project when it is evaluated.

Monitoring is a regular checking of how a project or an initiative is going.

Evaluation is a review of the project at a specific stage or at the end of setting it up.

Assessing changes in the community

Key questions to ask when monitoring our project

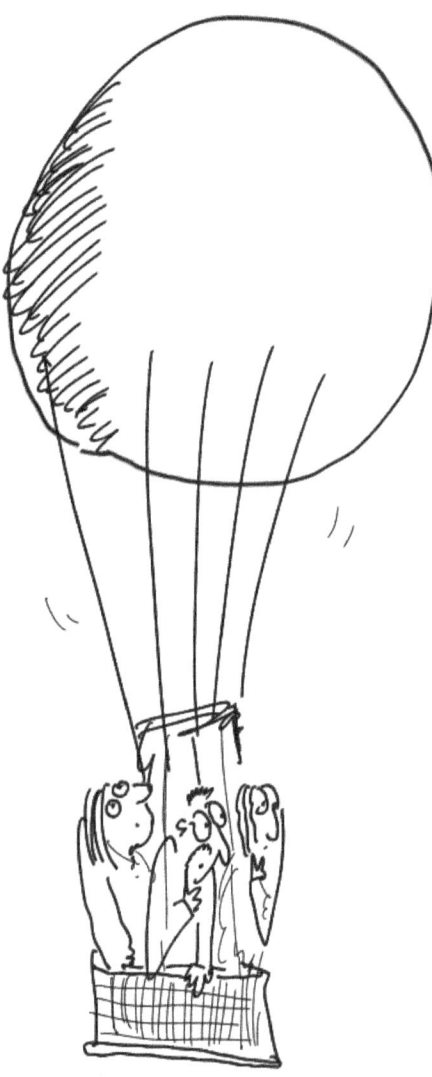

Are we doing what we said we would do?

If not why not?

What are the barriers and how can they be addressed?

Are we making a difference?

Is there anything we need to do to improve how we are running this project?

If you do not ask these questions regularly, you may find yourselves going in a direction you did want to go.

Are we doing what we said we would do?

It's important at regular intervals to look at the original plan the group made so they can check that the project is going in the right direction. A good way to do this is for the group to put up the original balloon picture to aid discussion about how everything is going.

Activity: Timeline of the project

On a large piece of paper, ask the group to draw a straight horizontal line across the middle. Put the date the project started at the beginning of this line and the current date at the other end of the line. Then the group should draw another line from one date to the other marking the highs of the project above the line and the lows below it.

When the line is drawn you can then have a discussion. Ask the question did we do what we said we would do?

Then discuss the highs

Are your highs related to your original plans?

What made these things go well and what can you build on?

Don't forget to take time to celebrate the good things?

Then discuss the lows

Why did these things happen?

Are there any lessons that can be learned for the future?

Keep a record of your timeline so that you will be able to show it to the community committees and to the community.

Are we making a difference?

To answer this question, we need to look at a range of tools which gather both quantitative (figures, data) and qualitative (stories, anecdotes, changes in attitudes) information. This information should be gathered on a regular basis throughout the life of the project. This same information can then also be used to evaluate the project when it has been completed or reached a significant point.

Activity: Stories of Significant Change

This is a good opportunity for everyone to contribute their experience of a community initiative or project and the changes they think it has made. It is done in the form of story telling which in many cultures has a great tradition.

Below are the key steps for guiding this activity.

Step 1

Invite as many people as possible who have been involved in the project or initiative and explain clearly that this is about them sharing their experience of the project and the effect it has had on the community.

Step 2

Remind them of how the project started, what the problem was it was trying to solve and the key stages that they went through to set up and run the project (it might be worth doing a timeline activity to help them remember the experience).

Step 3

Get them into small groups to discuss the following questions:

1. How are you involved in the project?
2. What changes have you experienced?
3. Which changes are significant to you?

Step 4

Invite each of the members of a small group to share a story about the project and why it was significant for them. They should think of a title for the story and these should be written on cards with the key points of the story and why it is significant written below.

Step 5

When all the stories have been told, place the cards on a blackboard or a large wall and try to group them into common themes and then discuss which themes or particular stories best reflect the change that has happened in the community.

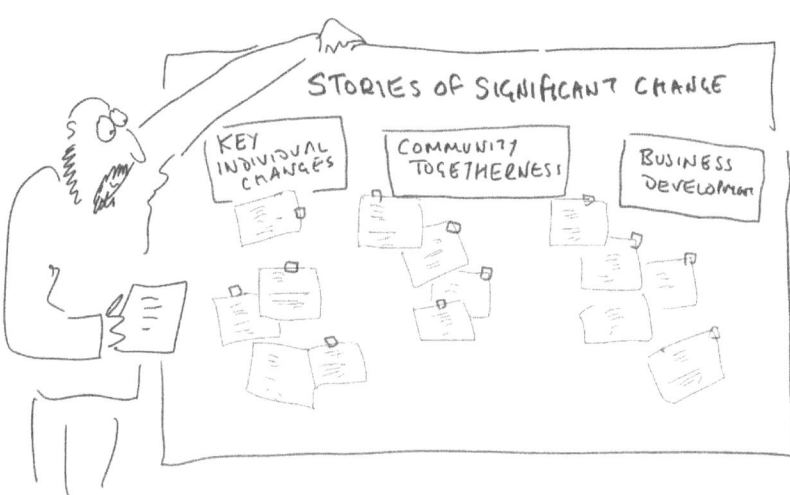

Is there anything we need to do to improve how we are running this project?

Here are two tools to use when answering this question.

Choose which is most appropriate.

Activity: The bicycle

This is a good tool to use when thinking about how your group is working together.

Think of the three different parts of a bicycle listed below.

Consider each part in turn and ask the following questions:

Brakes

What should we stop doing because it is not helping the project?

Chain

What should we continue doing because it is going well?

Pedals

What should we start doing because it would help the project?

Activity: Team Review

This is simply five questions to ask on a regular basis throughout the project:

1. What is your group doing that is helping the project?
2. How are they doing it?
3. What things are hindering the completion of the task?
4. What would you do differently?
5. What are you learning about team effectiveness?

For both the bicycle and the team review think about different aspects of the project such as:

- How we are organising ourselves
- How we are sharing information
- How we are encouraging people's contributions
- How we are getting feedback from stakeholders
- How we are managing our finances

Mosaic Creative

We are a small training consultancy, specialising in the use of drama, cartoons and illustrations to enhance learning and development. Our approach is about provoking a reaction, communicating ideas, exploring meaning and unlocking the creative potential in others.

Jackie Mouradian

Jackie is a professional actor, script writer and facilitator, working with both the corporate and charity sectors, especially in the context of organisational change and development. She writes and performs in sketches relevant to the needs of the company or organisation. She also co-writes community development materials for use in urban priority areas in the UK as well as communities overseas.

Bill Crooks

Bill has worked with the not for profit sector for over 30 years, both in this country and overseas, running courses on a wide range of community development issues. He is an accomplished cartoonist and illustrator and uses these skills to powerful effect in his training courses and workshops. He has been involved in the use of the performing arts in training and facilitation for the last 10 years.

Tel: 0118 9611359
Email: bill@mosaiccreative.co.uk
www.mosaiccreative.co.uk